# The Lost Treasure
of
# Sir Francis Drake

*by John Thrower*

*Front cover:*
From the Hondius portrait of Sir Francis Drake 1583
Photograph Michael Turner

*Frontispiece:*
Sir Francis Drake by Marc Gheeraerts
Reproduced with permission of Plymouth City
Museum and Art Gallery

*Page 14:*
Title page of "Sir Francis Drake Revived"
Reproduced with permission of Plymouth City
Museum and Art Gallery

ISBN 0 9527620 0 5

Copyright © John Thrower 1996
Whetley Orchard, Powerstock, Dorset. DT6 3TG

The right of John Thrower to be indentified as the author of this work has been
asserted by him in accordance with the Copyright, Designs and Patents Act 1988.

Printed by Creeds the Printers, Broadoak, Bridport, Dorset. DT6 5NL

# The lost treasure of Sir Francis Drake

*A search for the site of the ambush of the Spanish mule train by Francis Drake, near Nombre de Dios, Panama, April 1573*

Following two reconnaissance voyages in 1570 and 1571, Francis Drake in a third voyage, established bases in Panama from which he attacked and captured Nombre de Dios in July 1572 but failed to take treasure. Now allied to the Cimmarones, escaped black slaves, he attacked a Spanish treasure mule train near Venta de Chagres, some 13 miles from Panama City in January 1573; this attack also failed to capture treasure. Now allied also with the French, a successful ambush was achieved near Nombre de Dios in April 1573. About half a ton of gold was taken, worth at least £3.5 million today. Some 15 tons of silver bars were buried near the site, and probably not all recovered by the Spanish at the time. Does some of Sir Francis Drake's lost treasure remain there still?

Together with Michael Turner, the author has made two journeys to Panama, April 1993, March/April 1994, in order to visit various locations associated with Francis Drake's raid in 1572-3. In April 1993, 420 years after the ambush, we explored the Camino Real, the old Spanish trail, walking inland from Nombre de Dios. We found a likely area, near a river, where the ambush may have occurred. In 1994 we examined the area in more detail, and penetrated further inland to explore other candidate ambush sites suggested by E. Webster. This visit confirmed our 1993 identification as the most likely site for the ambush.

Reasons for the identification, the contemporary English and Spanish accounts and our exploration of the area are described and discussed.

*Sir Francis Drake*

# Contents

|  | | Page |
|---|---|---|
| **Chronology** | | **6** |
| **Introduction** | | **7** |
| **Historical Background** | | **10** |
| | Reason for Drake's raid 1572/3 | |
| | The Camino Real and old Nombre de Dios | |
| | "Sir Francis Drake Revived" | |
| | English, French and Spanish accounts of the ambush | |
| | Recovery of Treasure by the Spanish | |
| **Searching in Panama** | | **28** |
| | Nombre de Dios today | |
| | Walking inland 1993 | |
| | Walking inland 1994 | |
| **Discussion** | | **47** |
| | Distances | |
| | The River Campos | |
| | Route of the Camino over and beyond the River Campos | |
| | Nature of the terrain at the ambush site | |
| | The Ambush site | |
| **Conclusions** | | |
| | Further exploration | **54** |
| **References** | | **56** |
| **Maps** | | **57** |
| A1 | The Isthmus in 1572 | |
| A2 | The Isthmus in 1572 | |
| B | Nombre de Dios in 1572 | |
| C | Nombre de Dios today | |
| D | PANAMA today – the area of the Camino Real | |
| E | Nombre de Dios River – inland | |
| F | Junction of Nombre de Dios and Juan Miguel rivers | |
| G | Nombre de Dios River – further inland | |
| H | The Ambush Site 1573 | |
| **Appendix** | | **66** |
| | Amount and value of Gold and Silver on the Mule Train | |

# Chronology

| | |
|---|---|
| 1540/3 (about) | Francis Drake born at Crowndale, near Tavistock, Devon |
| 1547 | Edward VI King of England |
| 1549 | Drake's family driven out of Devon by Catholic rising |
| 1553 | Mary Queen of England |
| | Mary married Phillip of Spain |
| 1558 | Elizabeth Queen of England |
| 1562 | John Hawkins' first slaving voyage |
| 1566-7 | Drake sailed in Lovell's voyage to Spanish Main |
| 1567-8 | Hawkin's third slaving voyage |
| | Drake in command of Judith |
| | Battle of San Juan de Ulua |
| 1569 | Drake married Mary Newman |
| 1570 | Pope Pius V excommunicates Queen Elizabeth |
| | Drake's first reconnaissance voyage to Isthmus |
| 1571 | Drake's second reconnaissance voyage to Isthmus |
| 1572 | Ridolfi plot to assassinate Elizabeth |
| 1572-3 | Drake's raid on Panama |

# Introduction

To cross the Atlantic to the West Indies, sail the Caribbean to the Spanish Main, to set up bases under the noses of the Spanish, to capture Nombre de Dios, to climb a great tree on the Isthmus and view both oceans, to waylay a Spanish mule-train and sail home again loaded with treasure: these exploits of Francis Drake and his young crew are the stuff of history and adventure and have fired the imagination of so many over the years since 1573. Hot steamy jungle, brilliant blue sea, beautiful sailing ships, tropical islands, skirmishes with bow and arquebus, gleaming gold and silver bars: who can resist such romantic stories which are fact and not fiction, and take their proper place in the history books.

Yes, in the history books, and of course, that is as far as most readers are able to follow them. Later, there was so much more; the circumnavigation in 1577-80; conducting official English raids on the Spanish Empire and the battle with the Armada in 1588. But these early expeditions to Panama hold the most fascination for me, when the young Francis Drake was hardly known, when he was in sole command, when he was at his very best in dash and daring, and when he overcame amazing disasters and disappointments. Much of the detail was not known in his own day since it was not published until "Sir Francis Drake Revived"[1] appeared in 1626. Much was doubted as seeming more like fiction than fact. I first read of them in J A Froude, "English Seamen in the Sixteenth Century"[2]. He doubted much, the Professor of History at Oxford, but nevertheless aroused much interest. A true believer was Sir Julian Corbett[3] who also wrote an exciting novel about Drake's 1572 raid on Panama[4].

However, when Irene Wright[5] translated and published the relevant Spanish records in 1932, which had lain dormant in Seville for so long, much detail which had sometimes been taken as the boasting of Francis Drake was confirmed; his capture of Nombre de Dios for example. Here it is worth quoting from Irene Wright's own preface; page viii,:

> "... the reader is invited to study the story of Drake's attack on the pack train at Campos River, Nombre de Dios (April 1573), as told in *Sir Francis Drake Revived* and corroborated in Documents Nos 24, 31, etc., and ask himself whether he can reasonably doubt that the event occurred as the book relates; and finally, whether in any work of fiction (classic or "thriller") he has read anything to surpass

this tale, in diversity of incident, in vividness of description; or in the portrayal of character." .....

All this confirmed detail finds its place in newer accounts written since 1932. As examples one can give A E W Mason[6], J A Williamson[7], E Bradford[8], G M Thompson[9] and most recently J Sugden[10]. They are all well worth reading for background. Each author in his own way draws useful conclusions from the material.

Yes, all in the history books. But I wanted to go to the Isthmus, to visit these remote coastlines and locations, to see what they are like today. Can Drake's secret harbours be found, can the Camino Real be traced, what has happened at Nombre de Dios since it was destroyed in 1596? Can one, by a proper study, find the site of the mule train ambush? Can, even now, traces of this ambush be found? These and other questions ran through my mind. I had the time, having now ceased to work full-time for an employer, but how to do it? Of course modern air travel makes a journey to Panama relatively simple, if expensive; but even today it is hardly a tourist destination. Travel to the more remote locations would be a different matter; reading accounts, such as "Operation Drake"[11], bring climatic difficulties and possible health hazards to the fore. The project would be very much a back-packing adventure; Spanish would need to be spoken; boats and small planes would have to be hired, money would be needed in remote areas. Certainly a like-minded companion would be essential.

In 1991, while puzzling these questions, I came across an article in the *Daily Telegraph* about Michael Turner and his journeys all over the world to visit and photograph locations associated with the life of Sir Francis Drake – he was, as he entitles his project, travelling in *"Drakes Wake"*. We corresponded and met. Our interests coincided. Michael had much experience, health, strength, tremendous enthusiasm and spoke Spanish well. He had already visited Panama including Nombre de Dios and had looked inland from there. Luckily for me he planned further visits. In 1992, ill health prevented my travel with him to Drake's Port Pheasant, Port Plenty and Fort Diego (Map A1). In 1993 I was fit enough to join Michael, and owe him so much for the opportunity to make these exciting expeditions. We travelled extensively over the remote and very beautiful north-west coast of Panama, including the island of Escudo de Veragua, by small plane and boat. We visited Nombre de Dios and walked inland over the Camino Real. In 1994 we returned to visit Port Pheasant, saw most of the superb north-east coast by plane and boat and more of the Camino Real. On this part of the trip we were joined by Sue Jackson, a lifelong student of Francis Drake and History teacher. We mounted a 3-day expedition inland from Nombre de Dios to confirm our 1993 findings about the site of the mule-train robbery. This account will give detail, impressions and findings mainly on that single topic. But before doing so it is necessary to recapitulate some historical background of the reasons behind Drake's Raid, of Nombre de Dios, of the Camino Real and of the English and Spanish accounts of the ambush in April 1573.

# Historical Background

### The reasons for Drake's raid in 1572-3

Francis Drake was about 30 when he sailed out of Plymouth Sound on 24 May 1572 in two small ships: the Pascha, 70 tons and the Swan, 25 tons. Apart from one man of 50, all the crews were under 30 and all volunteers. This was certainly his fifth and possibly his sixth voyage to the Spanish Main and one that he had planned and prepared for very carefully "with intent to land at Nombre de Dios". Why? There is a considerable historical background which cannot possibly be covered here. The books referred to, deal with this in their various ways. To simplify matters we can do no better than to read his own words giving the reason; he was looking for recompense from Phillip II of Spain[1]:

> "The one being in his owne conceit the mightiest Monarch of all the world, the other an English Captaine, a meane subject of her Majesties. Who, besides the wrongs received at *Rio de Hacha* with Captaine *John Lovell* in the yeares 65 and 66, having beene grievously indamaged at Saint *John de Ullua* in the bay of Mexico, with Captaine John Hawkins in the years 67 and 68, not only in the losse of his goods of some value, but also in his Kinsman and friends, and that by that Falshood of *Don Martin Henriquez*, then the viceroy of Mexico, and finding that no recompence could be recovered out of *Spaine*, by any of his own means, or by her Majesties letters, hee used such helpes as he might by two severall voiages into the West Indies ......"

Thus, in his earlier voyages, he had run up against the dubious Spanish claim to exclusive rights in the Indies and Americas, a claim backed by the Pope and covered by the Treaty of Tordesillas, 1494, which both the English and French found oppressive. Even peaceful trade was forbidden. The battle of San Juan de Ulua, to which Drake refers, proved as well, to be the turning point for many other Englishmen. Don Martin Henriquez, the new viceroy, had broken his agreement with John Hawkins and treacherously tried to seize the English fleet in harbour. Ships, lives and some profits of the voyage were lost. Drake and Hawkins were lucky to reach home at all.

Drake never forgot this and frequently reiterated this episode and loss as his reason for the seizure of Spanish property, including those seizures on his later circumnavigation. Drake had no commission for the 1572/3 voyage any more than did a number of other English and French Privateers who were operating on this coast at the time, although there is some evidence that he was backed by certain individual members of the Queen's Council. But, the voyage is picked out in importance for its contribution to all the later events in Francis Drake's career; this was the hinge, the turning point, the establishment of his fortune and made all else that followed possible.

**The Camino Real and old Nombre de Dios**

All the gold, silver, jewels and other products of Spanish South America were shipped to the City of Panama on the Pacific coast of the Isthmus. This was the fine old city, now called Panama Viejo, some 3 miles east of the modern Panama City (Map D). Today it is a well preserved ruin as the city was sacked by Henry Morgan in 1671. The Cathedral tower still stands, on the altar of which Pizarro prayed before his journeys to explore Peru.

From Panama the Spanish developed an old Indian trail into their mule-train route across the Isthmus to Nombre de Dios, the Camino Real (the Royal road) *via* Venta de Chagres on the Chagres river (Map A1). A second trail, the Cruces, led to Casa de Cruces further down the river towards the coast. The trade followed these two routes according to commodity and season, while imports from Europe travelled in the opposite direction. Heavy goods moved *via* Cruces and the river; treasure shipments were by land over the entire Camino, for security reasons, during the dry season, January to April/May, to Nombre de Dios from about 1530-1595 and to Porto Belo thereafter until the Spanish abandoned the route altogether. Starting as a muddy track about 60 miles long, it was later paved certainly as far as the Capirilla pass, before entering river passage. The journey normally occupied three days with way-stations for resting the mules of which there were more than 1500 organised into 28 trains. The amounts of silver transported were enormous. By the 1570's over half the export of American silver to Spain was travelling over the Camino Real. The rate was at least 5 million pesos per season – possibly about 75 tons per week. So a loaded mule train such as the one that Francis Drake intercepted would be arriving at Nombre de Dios almost every other day. Silver was a commodity and so was regarded quite casually; Thomas Gage[12] noted that "piles of silver bars lay like heaps of stones in the street" at Porto Belo in 1637.

There is little published about the Camino and few maps. Fortunately, Michael has corresponded with Edwin Webster, an American who had spent some 24 years in Panama up to 1977 and had spent his spare time studying the history and geography of the country. He has published some of his studies and we have, fortunately, a copy of his excellent account of everything known about the Camino, and his attempts to follow parts of it, so far unpublished[13]. From the point of view of the present study we were most interested in the last few miles to Nombre de Dios. Over the final section, after Capira the route follows the Pavos and then the Nombre-de-Dios rivers; the last part leaves the Nombre de Dios and is routed to the old city over hilly ground, following the ridges, quite unpaved, descending to enter Nombre de Dios at the South East corner. (Map B). There is only one contemporary description[14] of this final section of the trail: by Sir Thomas Baskerville the commander of the land forces on Drake's final expedition to Panama in 1595-6. He took 600 troops hoping to cross the Camino so as to capture the City of Panama. They were forced to turn back from the Capirilla Pass held by the Spaniards (Map A2 and D). Important for this study it is quoted in full for the first part of the journey, from Nombre de Dios:

.... "The next day we resting fytting ourselves as well as our means would give us leave for thatt so tedious and so troblesom a jorney, the myseris of which I protest was very greatt, for all of us nonn exceptid was forcid to cary nyn days bread with hym 40 bolletes his bandolyers of pouder his Armes and a pound and a half in his pockett. Thus lodid we sett forward, and our way we fownd in this sorte. The first league upon the Tope of a mountayn coveryd with wode so narow, that the breadthe was nottabove xxty fote, throughe which passag was cutte. which being clay with the contynuall going of their reekos (Recuas-mule trains) and daily falling of raine is so stary (dungy?) and fowle thatt every steps is above the knee. The next 2 leagues you take up the course of a ryver for the most part up to the girdell, att the entering of which the enymy attendid us thinking to have defendid the passag butt seing we enterid the ryver having geven us 2 saulvos of Harquesbusades retirid and we held one our Journey to the fote of the mountayn of Capyra wher we lodgid and thus endid our first days Travayle..." ...

Edwin Webster has also compiled an excellent paper about old Nombre de Dios, its history and demise[15]. Established in 1509, it was properly founded in 1520 and in full use as a port until it was destroyed by fire in 1596. Baptista Antonelli surveyed the city for Phillip II in 1587[16]. He describes a collection of wooden houses with about 30 in permanent use. The rest of the population was seasonal according to the timing of the treasure fleet. There must have been considerable spare capacity as the Alcalde Mayor recorded the moving-in of at least 100 troops in 1572[5]. Also the Governor's house, the Church and the treasure house were built of stone. No city walls have been described, but as there were constant threats from the Cimmarones, the city must have been capable of landward defence for security, especially during the shipment of so much treasure during the dry season.

Sketch Map B is an attempt to reconstruct the topography of 1572. It may be compared with present Nombre de Dios, shown in sketch Map C. There has been a very important change over the years. To quote Edwin Webster[15]

"when the Canal Commission's sand dredging operation was active in 1907-11, the remains of two Spanish ships were found, one buried eight metres under the sand about seventy-five metres from the present shore. Similarly, the morro, once on the seaside at the eastern end of old Nombre de Dios, is now over one hundred metres inland from the bay".

So in Map B the shoreline has been moved south more than 100 metres to bring it close to the site of the old city and the morro. Also the sandbars, caused by silt washed down from the rivers and the dredged inland lagoon have been removed. The fort had not been completed in 1572 as Drake found no ordnance there but there were guns on the beach platform which he disabled during his attack.

The Spanish fleet first unloaded at the entrance to the bay as Baptista Antonelli noted[16]:

"Ships which doe come to this place doe unlode halfe there commodities between the two ledges of rocks for there is but little water in the harbour"

This was the Tierra Firma fleet which would arrive when the rainy season ended in January. Goods would be unloaded and the treasure taken on board. The fleet would then return to Cartagena at the end of the dry season to load the pearls, gold, hides and cochineal which had been

# Sir Francis Drake

Reuiued :

## Calling vpon this Dull or Effeminate Age,
to folowe his Noble Steps for Golde & Siluer,

By this Memorable Relation, of the Rare Occurrances
(neuer yet declared to the World) in a Third Voyage,
made by him into the Weft-Indies, in the Yeares 72. & 73.
when *Nombre de Dios* was by him and 52. others
only in his Company, furprifed.

Faithfully taken out of the Reporte of Mr. *Chriftofer Ceely*, *Ellis*
*Hixon*, and others, who were in the fame Voyage with him.
By *Philip Nichols*, Preacher.

Reviewed alfo by Sr. *Francis Drake* himfelfe before his Death,
& Much holpen and enlarged, by diuers Notes, with his owne
hand here and there Inferted.

Set forth by Sr. *Francis Drake* Baronet
(his Nephew) now liuing.

AVXILIO. DI. VINO

SIC. PARVIS. MAGNA

## LONDON
Printed by *E. A.* for *Nicholas Bourne* dwelling at the
South Entrance of the *Royall Exchange.* 1626.

The title page of Sir Francis Drake Revived

concentrated there. It would then sail for Havana, link up with the Mexican Flota and return to Spain. Nombre de Dios had by this time settled for its long wait for the next fleet the following year.

After Nombre de Dios was abandoned, the site was returned to the jungle. In 1682 William Dampier[18] slept in the bay and commented that there was no sign that anything had been there. Still in 1807[19] there was no habitation. After some mining operations nearby, in the latter 19th and early 20th century, this site was still undisturbed. In the 1970's new settlers moved into the area clearing the site of the old city which had already been partially disturbed by the building of the airstrip in 1959 – now part of the new road. Surface archaeology in 1976 clearly established the site of the old city. Edwin Webster said that at that time:

> "the chance existed to do a thorough excavation of a relatively untouched 16th century colonial site – the site of a city that for over half a century was of great importance in the history of Panama and in the development of colonial commerce".

The authorities were alerted, and an attempt was made to get sponsorship from Spain. That opportunity has now been largely lost as I will describe in the account of my own visit to Nombre de Dios.

From the point of view of the present study we needed to be sure of the site of the old city so as to measure distances and timings of the walk from the "Panama Gate" at its south-east corner. Also of interest is the River Fato (or Factor's River) which flows into the eastern side of the bay (Map B). This river figures in Spanish reports of the mule train ambush.

Webster has also made several suggestions for the site of the ambush, both in his paper on Camino Real, and in correspondence with Michael. These will be described and discussed alongside our own findings.

## "Sir Francis Drake Revived"[1]

Francis Drake was a good publicist and this is fortunate indeed because as a result we have a remarkable narrative in vivid detail made up from the writings of those who took part. As Irene Wright says "*Sir Francis Drake Revived*" deserves a permanent and honoured place among the very best records of those amazing 16th century adventures out of which grew the sea-power of England". As may be seen from the title page, reproduced here, it was edited by Drake himself and prepared for presentation to the Queen on 1 Jan 1592. Although this was almost twenty years after the events described, the account was certainly put together much earlier than that.

By the time it was published, by his nephew, in 1626, Nombre de Dios was long abandoned. Fortunately, by the time the Spanish read it the events had sunk into history. The capture of Nombre de Dios, a remarkable feat, appears on the title page. Too remarkable for many and much disbelieved as mentioned above.

Drake had established his Port Pheasant the previous year 1571:

"which is a fine round bay, of verie safe harbour for all winds, lying between two high points, not past halfe a cables length over at the mouth, but within eight or ten cables length everie way, having ten or twelve fadome water more or lesse full of good fish, the soile also very fruitfull".

Michael Turner has established the identity of this bay. Bahia Zapzurro just inside the Colombian border near Cape Tiberon. (Map A1)

The location of Port Pheasant had been betrayed to the Spaniards and the following day after Drakes arrival, July 13 1572, he was obliged to co-operate with a second party of English privateers under Captain James Rance. A fort was built and thatched shelters for the crew – it was the rainy season. Three pinnaces were assembled and within a week they set off for Isla Pinos, the Isle of Pines (Map A), where later he constructed storehouses and as a magazine it was his "Port Plenty". On from there to the Islas Cativas, to the Rio San Francisco, and to the attack on Nombre de Dios on 29 July 1572 at 3 o'clock in the morning. In the taking of the town, very cleverly done, Drake was wounded in the leg; his crew were so concerned the attack was abandoned leaving the massive store of treasure in the town.

In view of the normal timetable of the Tierra Firme fleet it must be doubted if there was in fact much treasure in the town; the fleet had left some weeks before. Drake was not fully familiar with this timetable but learned more of it later when he allied himself to the Cimmarones. He was also, perhaps, unlucky for the composition and timing of the fleet did vary a good deal from year to year[20].

So, after the attack on Nombre de Dios he had a long wait ahead of him until early the following year. He established a safe and secret base at Fort Diego (Map A1); he and his men kept themselves supplied from

Spanish shipping and by the aid and trade with Indians and Cimmarones. They were kept occupied with many adventures including daringly entering the harbour at Cartagena. Many of his men died in a raging attack of yellow fever.

Two more parts of Sir Francis Drake Revived need to be quoted in full for the benefit of this study. Some details of the attack on the mule train near Venta de Chagres in January 1573 and of course the successful ambush near Nombre de Dios. By January 1573 the English and Cimmarones were ready to undertake a long march across the backbone of the country to the farthest part of the trail between Panama and Venta de Chagres (Map A2). During this march the famous incident occurred when Drake climbed a "good and great high tree" from which he saw both oceans – he prayed God to give him life and leave to sail an English ship in the South sea. And so they reached a point within two leagues of Venta de Chagres, where they lay in wait for the mule train of the Treasurer of Lima who was returning to Spain with his daughter at the end of his career. The train was of fourteen mules of which no less than eight were laden with gold and one with jewels. Drake and his men waited near the trail:

... "Being at the place appointed, our Captaine with halfe of his men lay on one side of the way, about fiftie paces off in the long grasse. John Oxnam, with the Captaine of the Symerons and the other halfe, lay on the other side of the way at the like distance but so farre behind that as occasion served the former Company might take the formost Moyles by the heads and the other the hindmost, because the Moyles, tyed together, are always driven one after another; and especially that if we should have need to use our weapons that night we might be sure not to endamage our fellowes.."...

Unfortunately, due to the foolishness of Robert Pike, surprise was lost, the Treasurer turned back to Panama, the attack had failed. A fortune perhaps double in amount to that later taken near Nombre de Dios had slipped through their fingers.

The detail quoted above is important, it shows the careful planning and the need to envelop the whole mule train front and rear at the same moment. This same careful plan would be needed again on the next occasion, but surprise was essential.

## The English account of the successful ambush

Twenty Frenchmen, led by Captain Le Testu and fifteen English, led by Francis Drake together with a number of Cimmarones, led by Pedro marched through the jungle, in April, towards Nombre de Dios inland from the coast. They had landed at the Rio Francisco, where they appointed their pinnaces to sail away and return to pick them up – "to be there the fourth day next following without any faile". Although it is just 5 leagues by sea between the Rio Francisco (now the Cuango) and Nombre de Dios, by the way they marched through the jungle, crossing a number of rivers, they found the distance to be more than seven; not at all surprising – marches are always longer than distances marked on a map. They were well experienced by this time but needed to exert a strict discipline of silence on the French. Now to quote direct from the account:

> "When we were come within an English mile of the way we stayed all night, refreshing our selves in great stilnes in a most convenient place, where we heard the Carpenters, being many in number, working upon their Ships, as they usually doe by reason of the great heat of the day, in *Nombre de Dios*, & might heare the Moyles comming from *Panama*, by reason of the advantage of the ground. The next morning, upon hearing of that great number of Bells, the *Symerons* rejoyced exceedingly, as though there could not have befallen them a more joyfull accident, chiefly having been disappoynted before. Now they all assured us we should have more gold, and silver than al of us could bear away, as in truth it fell out.
>
> For there came three Recoes, one of fifty Moyles, the other two of seaventy each, every of which caryed 300. pound waight of silver, which in all amounted to neere thirty Tun. We, putting our selves in readinesse, went downe neere the way to heare the Bels, where we stayed not long, but we saw of what mettall they were made, and tooke such hold on the heads of the foremost and hindmost Moyles that all the rest stayed and lay downe, as their maner is. These three Recoes were guarded with fortie five Souldiers or there abouts, fifteene to each Reco, which caused some exchange of Bullets and Arrowes for a time, in which conflict the French Captaine was sore wounded with hayle-shot in the belly, and one *Symeron* slaine. But in the end these Souldiers thought it the best way to leave their Moyles with us, and to seek for more helpe

abroad, in which meane time we took some paine to ease some of the Moyles, which were heaviest loaden, of their cariages. And, being wearie, wee were contented with a few bars and quoits of gold, as we could well cary, burying about fifteen Tun of silver, partly in the boroughs which the great Landcrabs had made in the earth, and partly under old trees which are fallen thereabout, and partly in the sand and gravell of a River, not very deepe of water. Thus when about this businesse we had spent some two houres, and had disposed of all our matters, and were ready to march backe, the very selfe same way that we came, we heard both horse and foote comming as it seemed to the Moyles, for they never followed us after we were once entred the Woods, where the French Captaine by reason of his wound, not able to travell farther, stayed in hope that some rest would recover him better strength. But after we had marched some two leagues, upon the French Souldiers complaint that they missed one of their men also, examination being made whether he were slaine or no, it was found that he had drunke much Wine and over-lading himselfe with pillage and hasting to goe before us, had lost himselfe in the Woods. And, as we afterwards knew, he was taken by the Spaniards that evening and, upon torture, discovered unto them where we had hidden our Treasure".

Just these few sentences encapsulate a thrilling episode. These same sentences contain important and significant points to consider:

Where were they?
They *rested on a hill* as they had the *advantage of the ground* to hear sounds both from Nombre de Dios and on the trail from Panama
This hill was *close to the Camino* – within an English mile of the way
They went *down* to the Camino
They were near a *shallow river* with *sand and gravel*

The mule train comprised *190 mules* linked together in each of 3 trains. Even allowing just a modest 10 feet (3 metres) between the head of one mule and the next, some space between trains for soldiers and muleteers, we soon reach 2,000 feet or about 600 metres, so it was probably longer. The description strongly suggests an ambush on a land trail. Francis Drake would never have visited this spot before but he would have discussed the project very carefully with the Cimmarones who knew every detail of the Camino. They must have chosen the most suitable place,

*19*

indeed perhaps the only place, where such an ambush could be properly mounted, a long level area, with a straight trail, where the attacking party could dispose itself hiding over a sufficient length of trail and at a signal – arquebus or whistle, attack the whole long train at once in a swift operation. Complete surprise was essential since they would not risk part of the train rushing forward or back. They would need to take up position quickly and quietly so the hill where they waited must have been quite close to the trail.

After the quick skirmish, and when the Spaniards had fled, they had some two hours to dispose of the treasure. The distance from Nombre de Dios needed to be covered twice by Spaniards retreating and returning with re-inforcements is governed by that time – perhaps ¾ hour each way with a ½ hour turnaround?

The amount of silver is specified pretty closely – it is not exceptional as may be seen from the discussion above on the Camino Real. If every mule carried 300lb silver the total is about 25 tons of which some 15 were buried. The amount of gold is not specified and the account is very coy about this. By implication they carried off all the gold and 10 tons of silver. This is very unlikely; even 80 men would find it extremely difficult to make away with 2 tons, so considerable silver must have been still in view and left in the road.

Drake would have mounted sentries in each direction so as to be warned of any approach. When sounds were heard coming from Nombre de Dios the party stopped burying silver, gathered up the gold and retreated by "the very self same way". The Spaniards "never follow us after we were once entered the woods". Perhaps this suggests a clear area at the ambush site rather wider than the 9 foot wide way of the Camino.

**The French Account**

An interesting account by André Thévet in the French records is quoted by John Sugden[10]. Thévet claimed to have interviewed Le Testus' men:

"Those who accompanied Captain Testu took as much as they could carry: even the slaves leading the charges (mules) encouraged them to do so, through hatred of the Spaniard, showing them where the gold was so that they should not play around with silver. There were plaques of gold like two kinds of seals from the High

Chancellery of France, some of Castillian ducats, others of pistoles".

Also, the French "interred some of this silver on a tiny island".

## The Spanish accounts of the ambush

For these, as explained above, we are all indebted to Irene Wright[5].

The Spanish were meticulous in these matters; individual sworn statements were taken from those involved, or who were witnesses. These were made to the local officials, or were intended for the local Audiencia, the court of the province, representing the Spanish Crown, or to the King himself. All carefully preserved in Seville, the statements in the words of those interviewed, bring a freshness and immediacy to the record.

There are 8 documents relating to the ambush. Too lengthy to be reproduced here, the main points which emerge are summarised in Table I.

The statements vary in detail but some points are common to more than one statement. The robbery was on *29 April*; the news of this reached Nombre de Dios about noon. The place was on the high road at the Campos river, the distance quoted from Nombre de Dios being either *one, about 1½ or 2 leagues*. Pack *trains* are mentioned, sometimes two and the number of mules was *"more than 100"*. The value of the pack train was more than *200,000 pesos* of which as much as *20,000 pesos* belonged to the King. The King's share was also quoted as *18,300 pesos gold*. The amount taken was between *30,000 and 100,000 all in gold*. The amount taken was also stated to be as much as *150,000 pesos* (Document 28).

The most specific statement, by the Alcalde Mayor of Nombre de Dios, is of the amount of the King's gold recovered. Eleven bars valued at 6,300 pesos. In other statements the amount recovered altogether is either vague or is given as 30,000 pesos (lowest) to 100,000 pesos (highest).

Some sentences in the statements vividly convey the event:

| | |
|---|---|
| (The Corsairs) | "Came in through the bush to the Panama Highway" |
| (The Corsairs) | "Appeared on the high road" |
| (The Corsairs) | "Attacked the pack trains from Panama" |
| (The Guards) | "Those who were nearest to Panama ran that way and those who were on the Nombre de Dios side ran into that city" |

# Table I

| Document No Name Date of Statement | Place of Robbery ** | Distance from Nombre de Dios | Value of Pack Train | Amount Taken | Amount Recovered |
|---|---|---|---|---|---|
| 23 Jorge Nunez de Prado April 1573 | River Campos | – | – | – | 30,000 pesos |
| 24 Cristóbal Monte early May 1573 | – | 1 League | >200,000 pesos | 30,000 pesos†† | – |
| 26 Royal Officials of Panama | On the High Road | about 1½ Leagues | – | >100,000 pesos all in Gold | – |
| 27 Royal Officials of Nombre de Dios May 13 1573 | On the High Road | 2 Leagues | – | more than 80,000 pesos in Gold | 6308 pesos Gold# |
| 28 City of Nombre de Dios May 14 1573 | On the High Road | 2 Leagues | – | 150,000 pesos in Gold and Silver | Certain amount of Gold and Silver |
| 30 Juan Bautista Manuel and Alvaro Flores Sept/Oct 1573* | On the High Road | 1½ Leagues | – | – | Quantity of Gold and Silver in Road |
| 31 Diego Calderon and Witnesses April 22 1574 | River Campos | 2 Leagues | >200,000 pesos | – | about 100,000 pesos† 6300 pesos Gold# |
| 38 City of Panama April 15 1577 | River Campos | 1 League | >230,000 pesos | 130,000 pesos in Gold | 100,000 pesos? |

\*      At Seville

\*\*      All give date of Robbery as April or 29 April 1573

\#      Value of King's gold recovered

†      Only one of Diego Calderon's witnesses gave this figure saying "he believed about 100,000 pesos was recovered"

††      belonging to the King

"The call to arms sounded in the town, people went out by land"

"We sallied forth on the road on foot"

"Diego Calderon selected Captain Berrio with some 20-30 men and with this party set out down the road on foot"

"With much difficulty because it was a very muddy bad road"

"Diego Calderon mounted a mule he met on the way that he might go more quickly"

"Found the pack trains in disorder with many boxes broken open"

"In the road they found a quantity of gold and silver"

"Found the wounded Captain who was killed and a Frenchman who fled and came to the Factor's River and saw the King's Negroes working on the dam"

"Went two leagues into the wilderness ..... found the Corsairs dropping gold and silver"

"Some Citizens made it an excuse to busy themselves more in stealing than defending"

There are some important points here. It is clear that the ambush was on land and that the retreating Spaniards and those returning travelled on foot. The trail was very muddy so progress was slow. There was gold and silver still lying about when they reached the site. The line of retreat (and therefore of approach) was in the area of the dam on the River Fato (Drake's "very self-same way").

There is a disagreement about the distance, so, is it possible, or justified, to evaluate these statements and to compare one versus another on some of the important points?

"The City of Nombre de Dios" quotes the maximum distance, 2 leagues, and are the vaguest about the amount recovered and give the maximum figure for the amount taken. Obviously this helps to make up their excuse for failing to catch the robbers and provide cover for citizens helping themselves!

The variation of distance quoted is large. There is a great deal of difference between looking for a place 3 miles or then 6 miles away. The three estimates of 2 leagues are essentially one estimate, two are repeats. So the distance reports must be unreliable – they cannot all be correct. However, since the Campos River is specified three times, this does help to sort out the distance question; together with the line of retreat over the Fato River.

*23*

The Panama officials who were furthest away and so less responsible, were the first to be specific about the amount taken.

Statement 31 by Diego Calderon the Alcalde Mayor and his witnesses (who all agree with him!) is made a year later in order to plead for his own preferment and tends to maximise the amount recovered. He sticks to his figure of 2 leagues which he stated a year before and so this is not surprising.

That gold was left lying about seems unlikely. Drake's party would hardly have taken the trouble to bury silver while gold was still untouched. Most likely, the gold recovered, as reported to the King, was that picked up from the two Frenchmen.

From the precise figures given for the King's gold recovered, it is possible to calculate the weight of a gold bar and from the total value of gold given, the weight of gold on the mule train. The calculations, based on the relative values of the gold peso and the Elizabethan £1 gold coin, and the amounts of gold present in these fine gold coins, are shown in the Appendix. From these the King's gold bars weighed 7lb each and 77lb of his gold was recovered. Taking 100,000 pesos as the value of gold on the mule train the same method shows that *1218lb of gold* was carried *or more than half a ton.* The value of this, as metal, today, is about £3.5 million. If all the gold had been in bars, there would have been some 170 and *a full load for four mules.* But some was in quoits (probably of similar weight) and some in coin.

Turning to the silver, 25 tons as reported by Drake would be worth, as metal, today, about £2.3 millions. Does this match the figure given by the Spaniards for the value of silver on the mule train? Since they were giving the silver, by inference, a value of 100,000 pesos would this be worth £3.5 million, as for the gold above? In modern terms, today, £3.5 millions of silver weighs about 37 tons. But then the value of silver goes up and down and the relative values of gold – silver also vary. The Spanish, seemingly, meant different values when quoting for silver or for gold in the same unit of currency. M. F. Keeler discusses this point[21] and determines a ratio of 55:42 gold versus silver value. On that basis the 100,000 pesos of silver would be worth not £3.5 but £2.7 millions, so, much closer to the £2.3 million above.

All these figures are not given for their precise value but for what they indicate about the Spanish versus the English reports – the conclusion is that for the amount of silver, at least, they are close!

What were all these silver bars like, and how many did Drake have to deal with? He states that the silver bars he saw in Nombre de Dios weighed between 35 and 40lbs. Silver bars recovered from the Nuestra Señora de Atocha, wrecked in 1621 off the Florida coast averaged 60lbs each, and these had travelled the Camino in their turn[22]. Silver bars used to pay Drake's ransom of Cartagena in 1585 were mostly 50lbs each[21]. In our case it is fair to choose 50lb as a working example, i.e. 3 on each side of a mule for a full load. Silver is almost as dense as lead: a 50lb bar would measure about 30cm x 7.5cm x 10cm, a difficult heavy object for a man to carry very far and there were more than 1,100 of them on the mule train! In order to hide 15 tons no less than 670 of them would have to be shoved down crab holes etc – Drake's men would not have spades with them – small wonder that a considerable amount was still lying around when the Spaniards returned.

**Recovery of treasure by the Spanish**

Drake's party would have been careful to make sure of all the gold, before troubling themselves with silver (p.24). This strongly suggests that the 77lb of gold, that the Spaniards did recover, was the amount being carried by the two Frenchmen captured. 35-40lb of gold would be quite sufficient for a man to carry, bearing in mind that weapons and food were also part of his burden, for a 21 mile march in jungle heat. Pro rata, the 1218lb of gold would need to be distributed between some 35 men; which meant that the English and French were fully burdened with gold alone. However, Report No. 38 (Table 1), made 4 years later, suggests that the gold may have amounted to 130,000 pesos or 1583lb. We do not know how many Cimmarones were in the party. They may have been occupied in carrying weapons and equipment; but could also have helped either with this extra amount of gold or with carrying silver. Even 40 Cimmarones would have had some difficulty with 1 ton of silver, 45 bars at 50lb each. All this demonstrates that at least 24 tons of silver, buried and unburied, remained at the site of the ambush when the Spaniards returned.

More than a fortnight after the ambush, Drake sent 12 English and 16 Cimmarones under John Oxenham, back to the site to recover treasure, and also possibly to rescue Captain Testu, though hope of this was remote by that time. This party later returned with 13 bars of silver and "some few quoits of gold"; a quantity which may have been considerably more than the description suggests, bearing in mind that the total haul was also previously described as "a few bars and quoits". The fact that this return expedition was kept secret from the French strongly suggests that the gold it recovered had been hidden by the English, near the ambush site, unknown to the French, and had eluded any search by the Spaniards. A recovery party of 26 men was clearly not, in any event, able to return with a significant amount of silver, so it was obviously planned as a "gold-recovery" expedition. Otherwise its despatch would have made no sense. Also, Oxenham may not have known all the places in which the French buried silver.

A Frenchman, who returned to the Rio Francisco, and was rescued by Drake, when he took Oxenham's party to that river, is quoted[1] as saying that 2,000 Spaniards and negroes had been employed to recover the silver from the site of the ambush by digging. Apart from sounding very unlikely, this effort is not confirmed in the Spanish reports (see below). John Oxenham's party also later reported that the area had been dug over for a mile around the site. Both these reports become rather suspect when it is realised that the Frenchman would not have known about such a search as he had quickly fled from the scene. Also the report, and its subsequent "confirmation" by Oxenham, would have provided a convenient cover against other treasure-seekers who might read Drake's account subsequently and follow later.

So, how much treasure did the Spaniards recover? Drake could not have been sure how much was buried since the English and French parties were working as much as 600 metres apart. But his figure of 15 tons (60,000 pesos) would mean that 9 or 10 tons (40,000 pesos) remained in full view for the Spaniards to collect up when they returned. The reports by local officials, Nos. 27 and 28 (Table I), made a fortnight after the ambush, when searches must have been complete, are vague about the amount recovered. These same officials would have been only too ready to claim credit for a major search by 2,000 men which had recovered all the silver. On the contrary, there is nothing in the reports to suggest that anything like that took place; looking at the appropriate wording in those reports we find:

27 "Best efforts to find gold either on the highway or on the trail

the corsairs left, have availed to recover only 10 gold bricks worth 6308 pesos"

28 "Gathered up a certain amount in bars of silver and gold which the corsairs abandoned because they could not transport them"

These statements also throw doubt on Report 31, by Diego Calderon and witnesses, made a year later, when one witness said

"he thought about 100,000 pesos had been recovered" (Table I).

Report 38, made four years later, may well be a repeat of Report 31 in its claim that 100,000 pesos was recovered.

The most straightforward statement about recovery comes from the Report 28 by the City Council of Nombre de Dios. This provides the only estimate of the amount of silver the Spanish thought was missing. They state that Drake took 150,000 pesos in gold *and* silver. Now, we know that the maximum estimate for gold is 130,000 pesos, then the City Council thought he had taken, at least, 20,000 pesos in silver. Putting this the other way round, they cannot have recovered more than 80,000 pesos.

Summarising: Drake's party made off with about 1 ton of silver; the Spaniards picked up about 9 tons and dug up another 10 tons. So, about 5 tons, or 225 bars, remained hidden after the search.

This discussion, highly speculative, nevertheless rests on the official statements and figures, given at the time, and sensible consideration of how much Drake's party could have transported. Undoubtedly, a close search must have been mounted. It may not have been pushed to its limit, simply for practical reasons, and also taking into account the casual attitude which developed towards silver[12] when such large quantities were seen every day. The Spanish were also inured to the loss of treasure after raids by the Cimmarones. The balance of probability is that a significant quantity remained hidden, near the site, even after Oxenham's return visit.

One would imagine and like to think that a number of these large silver bars still lie buried there, near the River Campos!

# Searching in Panama

## Nombre de Dios today

"Why on earth would you want to visit Nombre de Dios?" asked Colonel Glenn. Michael and I were paying a call at the British Embassy in Panama City at the end of my first visit to Panama in 1993. We were able to explain our reasons readily enough. But, if one travelled all the way up to the North Coast on hot, tiring and slow roads simply to visit the modern village, then Colonel Glenn would have a point.

Modern Nombre de Dios surrounds an inland lagoon left by the Panama Canal Commission's sand dredging operation, at the eastern end of the bay (Map C). Typical of many of the villages in the region, though considerably superior to some of them, it has a square with a scruffy "supermarket" and bar. Large signs advertise "Atlas" and "Panama" beers. Cheap modern buildings share the site with shanties and shacks interspersed with palm trees. There is even a "hotel" from which Michael recommended we keep clear, unless wishing to be eaten alive with mosquitos. Further along the coast road is a school. There is a general air of lassitude. It is hot. However, the people are very friendly and helpful.

The sign at the edge of the village reads:

Bienvenido a Nombre de Dios
Fundador:   Diego de Nicuesa   Fundacion 8 de Marzo de 1509
Patrono:   Torrbio de Mogravejo, Arzobispo 1538-1606

A sense of the history, but then they are referring to the old city which no longer exists.

My first sight of Nombre de Dios was from the air and conveyed a quite different impression. We had hired a small plane from the King Crab company in Panama City. They had obligingly removed one door so that we could take photographs with a clear view from the passenger seat side. Michael occupied this seat while I sat in an extra seat fitted behind. We flew over old Panama City and then northwards over the route of the Camino Real as far as Capirilla at the head of Lake Alajuela (Map D). We then turned to fly over the coast, past Porto Belo and Islas Bastimentos. From there we turned into Nombre de Dios Bay with its beautiful semi-circular sand beach, fringed with palm trees and a backdrop of jungle clad hills. A superb setting. The famous bay of Sir Henry Newbolt's poem, the bay where the annual treasure fleet gathered, where Pizarro landed and where Drake's pinnace rowed in. The modern village can have barely changed the view.

But, we were amazed to see a large black patch of land at the western end of the bay near the straight road which was formerly the airstrip. There were cranes, temporary buildings and a pontoon jetty jutting into the bay. We could not linger so investigation would have to wait until we arrived on foot.

Our visit to Nombre de Dios in 1993 was at the end of our travels from Drake Bay on the Pacific coast of Costa Rica and all along the north west coast of Panama. I had survived these adventures well and was enjoying the heat rather than finding it tiresome. We drove up by taxi from Panama City; this may sound luxurious but was an economical means of travel for two people at $5 per hour! A long hot drive along the very noisy and busy road to Colon, turn off at Sabanita, a noisome junction of shanties, on to the side road leading up to Porto Belo, eventually gaining fine views of the coast; passing Bahia Buenaventura and then the famous Spanish Forts in Porto Belo harbour. We finally travelled slowly along the rough, winding, hilly dirt road to Nombre de Dios (Map D) arriving in the dark, by this time I was used to sudden darkness after 6pm. We were readily put up for the night by a family with a house, which was still being built on the beach, at the western edge of the village. A very pleasant spot; the cooling sea breeze was welcome and meant the virtual absence of mosquitos. I struggled with my mosquito net for the first night but on the second night under the thatched roof I slept without it. A timeless view of the moonlit bay with fireflies circling overhead in the palm trees.

The next morning Michael showed me the hill on the east side of the old city (Map B) on which the shape of the Spanish earthworks were still clearly to be seen. The very "platform without any ordnance" which Drake found in 1572, and from which a "cannon which brake" was fired at him in 1595[23]. As we climbed up the slope to the top, I spotted a piece of broken cannon on the path. Michael had seen this before and knew it to be part of the very "cannon which brake" and had originally been on the top of the fort; we hid it for safety. Later I saw the main part of this cannon in a farmhouse garden. James Tumlin had found this cannon with a metal detector on the fort in 1976.[15]

There is a superb commanding view of the famous bay from the top of the fort. Modern changes are virtually unnoticed. One can gaze around at a beautiful unchanged scene.

From here we set off for our walk along the Camino described below. Later in the day, we returned to the village from the river, hot and tired after a 12 mile inland hike. We realised with horror that the large black area we had seen from the plane next to the road at the edge of the village was a compound set up by a mining company digging for manganese. It was evident they had cleared the site of the old city having bulldozed off the surface, pushing this back to form the banks of their slurry lagoon at the rear of the compound. They were closing for the night. Just as we were leaving Nombre de Dios the next day, following our visit to the river Cuango along the coast, we had a short time whilst waiting for the bus to Porto Belo, to examine the piled earth. We found many artefacts which looked like 16th century pottery etc. I found a wine-or-olive jar neck with characteristic markings, which has subsequently been identified as 16th century Spanish by the British Museum. Michael also found some large pieces of pottery, on the other side of the road to the west, around palm oil trees.

*The unique opportunity for 16th century colonial archaeology, identified by Edwin Webster in 1976 has been lost.*

On return to Panama City, we visited the National Museum so as to tell the senior archaeologist there about this destruction. Unfortunately we could not detect any real concern on his part and we had no confidence that he would, or perhaps could, do anything about it.

**Walking inland 1993**

Following the dirt road which leads to the southern outskirts of the modern village, before reaching the area of the inland lagoon (Map C), one takes a turn to the right along a side track to the south. To the east rise the wooded slopes of Cerro La Gloria. We passed a few houses where enquiries reassured us that we were, indeed, walking the "Camino Antiguo". On a hot morning the sun was already beating down fiercely; rain in the night had made the surface wet in spite of this still being the "dry-season" or "summer". We were glad to have had plenty to drink before setting off and to have full drink bottles; we were also glad to have left our heavy rucksacks in the house on the beach. The path soon lost sight of the village climbing a long gentle slope; the hill marked 34m with a radio mast was to our right (Map C). Turning to look back north, gave a view of the bay above the tree tops; one could imagine this to be a welcome sight to muleteers in the old days, the very last stage of a long, difficult overland journey from Panama, not without danger.

The track consisted of an orange-brown hard soil with a clay content – superficially sticky, but hard underfoot because of the dry season; fringed with coarse grass and indented into the slope like a narrow sunken lane. Some of the coarse long grass had been cut and laid to dry – for thatching perhaps? Insufficient knowledge prevents my naming the various types of tropical trees and vegetation. Hot and humid but, surprisingly, neither flies to bother us nor any undergrowth to impede progress. Old the trail might be but it is well used. Soon surrounded by trees we were walking through woodlands which could almost be described as jungle bordering each side of the trail.

We reached the top of the long slope where the trail divided, here we met two men wielding machetes. In answer to our enquiry they said they did not know which fork we should follow; luckily we knew from the map[17], which Michael was following by compass, to turn left. We then descended a long slope, now through thick jungle on each side, there was a small stream at the bottom with a few logs thrown over to help one over the orange clay. Hot, humid and perfectly quiet.

We forged on, determined to keep walking without any halt so that we could time our walk over a recognised distance. The trail climbed again quite steeply, and after this kept mostly on ridges with the occasional turn, minor climb and minor descent. Quite comfortable, especially in the shadier regions, I was genuinely enjoying the walk in spite of the growing heat.

Fascinated by where we were walking, my thoughts strayed to those who had travelled this way before; Pedro Arias de Ávila the first governor of Tierra Firma; Francisco Pizarro the conqueror of Peru; muletrains with the lash of the whip on the slaves' backs; and, finally, Thomas Baskerville and his men on their desperate march. The ridges we were on were often quite narrow, as one could see, by occasional areas cleared of trees by slash and burn which dropped away on one side or the other – thus fitting Baskerville's description "that the breadthe was nott above xxty fote". We were certainly having an easier time than he did. He was still in the rainy season with "every step above the knee"; there was some red mud

*31*

creeping into my sandals which caused them to slip a little, but nothing worse.

Edwin Webster walked this trail for about a mile; he states that "cuts from over sixty years of heavy-mule traffic from the first shipment from Peru to the shift to Porto Belo should still be there to be found". Some distance beyond this first mile we found a "cut" as the trail ascended a short steep slope. Very reminiscent of a "Devon Lane" in miniature but only just wide enough to take mule traffic; brought to mind were descriptions of parts of the Camino which were just wide enough for a horseman with the vegetation on each side brushing his shoulders! Our confidence that we were still following the Camino was maintained. I imagined the untold millions in treasure which had slithered down this very slope and the laden mules struggling up sometimes carrying heavy jars of mercury for the silver mines or, more pleasantly, wine or oil. The Spaniards hurrying to the ambush – Faster! – because of worries about the King's treasure – Slower! – because of worries about the Corsairs and the feared Cimmarones, and all the while silver bars were being buried!

There now follows a longer section, a narrow ridge on higher ground where we could see well inland as the trees had been felled in an area to our right (west). The trail ahead could be seen to make a turn almost 90° to the right and rise to a tree clad hill. On reaching these trees the trail, swinging left, began to descend towards an extensive plain. Another "cut" to be negotiated as we walked down; we could see fields of cattle and a small river crossing the trail ahead of us. We felt we had reached a significant place, we had been walking for 1 hour, 10 minutes – though it seemed much more!

After the descent from the hills, the track ran gently down north to south to a muddy ford crossing the small river which was flowing east to west at the ford. About 2-3 metres wide with meanders; deeper pools on the outside curves with shingle banks on the inside. The river had come from the south with some higher ground to its east; now, at the ford, on to the west edging the higher ground on its north bank with a large fenced cattle field to its south. There were trees dotted along the banks. Far too small for the Nombre de Dios, which was out to the west, it was clearly its first tributary as shown on the map (see sketch Map E). Was it the river Campos we wondered? Webster had said that it might be.

Ahead the trail was running south over level ground, fenced on each side, river to the east, large level field to the west. Further ahead was more level ground so we were confident we had reached the extensive level area shown on the map (Map E & G) where the river Nombre de Dios makes two major 90° turns, first flowing east and then flowing west-north west.

Having rested at the ford, we looked across to the rising ground to the east. Climbing through the barbed wire fence and crossing a small stream which ran into the river near the ford, we climbed the hill. Very hot, so I put up my folding umbrella to act as a sunshade, this was midday, the sun burned down from vertically overhead. Michael was ahead of me, he shouted back that he could hear the mining machinery from the site of old Nombre de Dios but I could not from lower down. When I reached the top I listened carefully. Faint sounds without a doubt, and the wind was favourable. We looked at each other with the same thought – Drake's men hearing the carpenters working at Nombre de Dios in April 1573! We sat on the hill which, though hot, had a pleasant breeze, the wild orange trees providing ready refreshment. The flat top of the hill could easily have accommodated Drake's men!

During the course of that hot day we made various sorties from the ford to explore the area (Map F). We walked west all along the small river to check that it did indeed join the Nombre de Dios; the large river proved a beautiful sight with long wide reaches and trees alternating with grassy banks. Being the dry season the low volume river varied its course between long shingle banks; beautifully refreshing clear water. From the junction of the river and back along the bank we came to one of the major sharp turns in the river. From here the fence and trail ran east for a distance, whereupon it forked, one fork followed a south-east course across level ground to the west of the small river; the other fork, the main trail, turned north to reach the ford again (Map F).

From the hill with the orange trees we walked around on the high ground skirting the east side of the plain. There were several reasons for this. We would have a good view of the plain; we would be following more closely a route Webster had suggested for the Camino and we would be able to listen for sounds from Nombre de Dios at greater distance.

The whole level area appeared to be a "flood plain" of the Nombre de Dios river with the tributary running through as on the map (Map F). Level and grassy, dotted with various tropical trees, inhabited with cattle of the "African type". Flocks of white cattle egrets were around, the occasional parrot could be seen. All very calm, peaceful and hot. In fact, very hot – my sunshade was essential. Estimating the size of the plain from the map and by observation, there were several directions where a 600 metre mule-train could cross and be ambushed in a single attack – again, was this tributary the Campos river? Sitting on the next major hill on the east side we could not hear sounds from Nombre de Dios; also it was steep-sided and narrow – perhaps less suitable to accommodate Drake's party. We had not seen any signs of a trail on this east side.

We climbed down slowly to the small river; the level fields area was hard and dry at this time of year. At a ford where we crossed the river, refreshing ourselves with a dip, a farmer appeared holding a machete. However, he was very friendly and conducted us up to his house on a nearby ridge; Señor José González and family. The attractive wooden farmhouse with a patio, thatch roof and shaded verandah gave us a welcome rest. We were given refreshing drinks and a tasty meal of chicken stew.

Later, with José we walked again along a ridge approximately southwards from the farmstead. Gradually we worked our way eastwards from the high ground down again into the ravine of the small river. We were now near to the general area nominated by Edwin Webster as one of his candidate sites for the ambush (Map G). Here the tributary river was smaller with mud rather than gravel. The ravine was steep-sided with little space to organise and dispose attackers along a sufficient length of trail. Moreover, we doubted that the trail would have followed this route. After walking back towards the farm through José's maize and bean fields, and along by the small river, we rewarded José for his services. We told him we would like to return, with more time to explore, on another occasion.

Working our way across the plain from the farm ridge we reached the Nombre de Dios river having decided to return to the coast by this route. The path on one bank, or the other, on a central shingle bank or on islands, meant crossing and re-crossing the river. A beautiful landscape, now just pleasantly warm in late afternoon.

At the village we sat in hammocks at the café on the beach, which had opened for the benefit of the manganese miners, sipping cool drinks and looking out across the brilliant blue water of the bay. We had many memorable impressions from a truly amazing day. These needed to be

*José Gonzalez*

*The Farmhouse*

carefully thought through. There were inconsistencies between what we had observed and the guidance from the map.[17] Notwithstanding these we were buoyed up with what we had seen because in many ways the area around the farm fitted the requirements of the ambush site. A small river running through fields. The word for fields in Spanish is Campos.

While at the farm we had a good discussion with José who had proved extremely helpful. Before departing, and without any prompting, we asked him the name of the small river. Although the reply was not the one hoped for, we were amazed by what he said:

*The small river was called Juan-Miguel – the John-Michael!!*

Rivers chop and change their names in Panama and have very frequently changed their names since Colonial days. We were not at all disappointed but, rather, took the name to be a good omen for our search.

**Walking inland 1994**

For Easter 1994, we wished to return to Nombre de Dios, walk southwards again so as to check our findings. A great deal had been seen and discovered in one day, but we needed more time in the area; we hoped to stay at the farm of Sr González for two nights so as to afford three days for investigation. This should enable us to:

Check distances, timings and details of the area versus the map. Penetrate further down the valley of the Nombre de Dios to the junction with the Pavos river – another candidate ambush site suggested by E Webster.
Look for 16th century artefacts or treasure in the area especially in the Juan Miguel river.

To look for antiquities in Panama requires a permit and supervision by the Department Patrominio Historico. When we visited the British Embassy in 1993, they had been very ready to assist us so as to arrange for just such a project with the Government of Panama. However, we had been more than disappointed by the lack of interest shown by the very officials at the National Museum, who would be given the task of supervision of any search we might make. No concern had been shown to protect known antiquities, let alone those for which the location was not even known. We did not wish to be slowed by administrative bureaucracy until we were sure of our findings and knew that there was something worth looking for, especially as the time available for the present search was so limited. We decided to take a metal detector with us and gain the co-operation of Sr González to do some preliminary scouting. If we were lucky enough to find anything we would take up the matter of a comprehensive search with the Embassy and the Government.

On Sunday 27 March 1994 we arrived in Panama City in the evening. On Monday we were able to make arrangements for the remainder of our expedition including those for a flight to Puerto Obaldia near the Colombian border so that I could visit Drake's Port Pheasant. Michael had very kindly agreed to travel there with Sue Jackson and myself.

Michael had already made arrangements to borrow a metal detector capable of working underwater, and by Monday evening we arrived in Nombre de Dios to stay at the same house on the beach. The family had made some more progress in the building of their house and were, once again, very hospitable.

Early on Tuesday, at about 7am, we set out along the Camino, this time with full backpacks. Cooler than 1993 for two reasons; earlier in the day and much cloudier. The walk along the trail was easier as the surface was perfectly dry; carrying heavy packs and a metal detector was compensated for by the cooler conditions. I made sure that I took photographs all along the route for my own records. There had been more forest clearance towards the end of the route over the hills, where the trail makes a major turn to the right towards the west-south west. Standing still to photograph this section of the trail, I could see the hill, where we had found the wild orange trees, in the background above the ridge ahead of me. Our walk to the Juan-Miguel river took 1 hour 15 minutes; we had taken a short rest from the weight of our packs back at the small stream in the valley.

We walked straight across the plain to the farm and met Sr José González again. He remembered us well. Yes, we were welcome to stay with him and his family; his biggest worry seemed to be that he could not offer us bedrooms because his various daughters, daughter-in-law and grandchildren were all there for the Easter holiday. Michael and I assured them that we would be quite happy to sleep on the verandah.

When we discussed our need to search for antiquities he immediately told us that this presented a problem; he had entered into an agreement with a man from Panama who was to search the whole of his land within his fences. We were fascinated but worried – we wondered who else wanted to search the area, and why? We expressed our disappointment and wondered if we could search the river itself – at this he relaxed and was more than happy to agree – we were pleased because this had always been our intention. While talking to José, just outside his farmhouse fence, looking out over the peaceful plain with the grazing cattle, we turned suddenly to see a large bright green snake coiled along the fence wire behind our backs. José swiftly despatched the snake with his stick.

We had always planned to look in the river, because with limited time, over a large area, it seemed the only certain place; we could not possibly mount a more comprehensive search. Drake had hastily buried silver *"in the sand and gravel of a river not very deep of water"*; we hoped this was in the Juan-Miguel. The most likely place to look was where we thought this river ran beside the trail, just before the trail reached the ford and entered the hills; whichever way the trail crossed the plain it would funnel into this section.

Without more ado, we returned down to the river with just our refreshments and the detector; we were very pleased that the weather was so much cooler than in 1993. Time was needed to become familiar with the detector and the reaction it made to metal objects under water. Panama Balboa coins deliberately hidden in the gravel under water were rediscovered with ease; the signal consisted of a note in the earphones which became almost unbearably loud close to any large metal object but was also sensitive to very small items such as small pieces of wire of which there were many which had come from the wire fences all around. When in close range a red light showed as well. Gradually skill was built up on recognising size, shape and depth of metal objects.

Working down the river Juan Miguel from where the trail divides (Map F) towards the ford. On a bright cloudy day with spells of sunshine, wading in a cool river under pleasant shady trees, we were enjoying conditions not unlike a warm English summer day. Humidity was low and insects notably absent.

Over the stretch the river meanders, thus tending easterly then westerly gradually covering distance north towards the ford. As noted the previous year there were shingle banks on the inside and deep pools on the outside of the bends. In the morning we were digging for objects with my plastic trowel (which had been a free gift stuck on the cover of Gardener's World!), but after lunch at the farm we were well equipped with José's spade. Besides the pieces of wire or scraps of corrugated iron, other objects found included a spoon, a battery and a large nail embedded in a piece of fence post. In one place we were excited to find an oblong metal object buried deep in muddy gravel, in a deep pool, which rang when struck with the spade. It proved to be the remains of a mattock or pickaxe head! Most of the day was spent covering this section up to about 20 metres from the ford.

Back at the farm José laughed with us at our "finds". That evening, after our wash in the river he took us to another spot, further down the western bank of the Nombre de Dios river, where a Colombian man had found some gold with a detector (Map F, point +). An absolutely beautiful evening; José tried out the detector in his indicated spot but found only a rusty nail!

After supper in the farmhouse, we wrote up our diaries by the light of flickering wicks burning paraffin; sometimes these would be blown out by the breeze plunging us into darkness. José loved to talk and would have continued for hours, but tired out, we needed our beds. Tomorrow José would take us to the junction with the Pavos river. The verandah was cool, making a pleasant sleeping spot, but later in the night a shift inwards was needed to shelter from wind and rain.

Aquilina González provided a good breakfast, after which we set out on foot crossing the high ground to the south west of the farm. Down again and across a small stream we were again in level fields near to the Nombre de Dios river. Many trees were dotted about; occasionally a large buttressed tree. Climbing again to another ridge we had a good view of a sweep of the river. We were working our way up the valley of the Nombre de Dios in a general south-south west direction on the east bank of the river, but taking "short cuts" to avoid the large bends (Map G). Down again, crossing more fields, we came to a part of the river with thick forest sloping up on each side. This made necessary a wading trip up a length of river from one shingle island, or bank, to another. At one point we tried to walk a jungle path on the west bank to avoid a deeper section of river, the path was so overgrown, steep and slippery that we were forced to abandon it and return to wade the river again which fortunately had a gravel base and was just about waist deep if one was careful to follow José's direction. Cameras, etc. were in small rucksacks high on the shoulder; José carried the metal detector well clear of the water.

I thought of Baskerville and his troops wading up this stretch of river "for the most part up to the girdell". They would have needed to hold up arquebus and powder well clear of the water; we were now doing the equivalent.

Clambering out of the river, across some more fields the route climbed over some steep cleared hills on the "west" bank to avoid some more bends in the river. Some fierce rain squalls hit us on this section. Down again to more fields near another farm; after crossing these we at last came to the junction of the Nombre de Dios and Pavos rivers (see Map G). The combined river and land walk had taken some 2½ hours.

We were now at a candidate site for the ambush suggested by Webster. The Pavos river flowed into the Nombre de Dios contributing an orange opaqueness to the clear water for some distance downstream. A large shingle bank island occupied the junction. The fields we had crossed were to the north and west. Thick jungle occupied each bank of the Nombre de Dios river upstream. Some metal detecting on the shingle bank and shingle island revealed no metal objects present in either.

Apart from other general considerations, which I will discuss later, the area was just too far away in walking distance, (although probably about two leagues from Nombre de Dios altogether) to fit the timescale for the ambush. Also we simply could not believe that sounds from Nombre de Dios could be heard at this long range.

José said he knew the farmer nearby and suggested we hire horses for the return journey – we very readily agreed! He went off to fetch them; I looked after all our kit while Michael walked a little further up the Nombre de Dios river to view Webster's remaining suggested site. He returned having concluded that it was even less likely than the river junction.

Then followed a memorable journey on horseback down the Nombre de Dios river to return to the farm. Relatively cool and shady because of tree cover, the horses made easy work of the river stretches and steady progress on the shingle banks, although riders needed to be on the alert to watch the depth of water and also so as to dodge overhanging branches, with which the horses seemed to delight in bringing one into contact. Occasionally there would be a fallen tree across the shingle or in the river; an important obstacle as even stepping over a smaller diameter near the end of the tree proved quite hazardous for a horse. At one point on the western bank we diverted from the river onto a well established short section of trail in order to avoid a deeper than usual pool, then re-entering the river. Apart from these minor problems the whole ride was a delight down this absolutely beautiful river – our struggles with the long walk in the morning were now amply rewarded. Nowhere was the river bed difficult for the horses. Often the legs of horse and rider were comfortably cooled by the refreshing water. One could readily appreciate why the Camino would take a river route over stretches where the conditions made this practicable. How much easier than any jungle trail. The muleteers must have quite enjoyed this section of the route as respite from other struggles. The Treasurer of Lima, no doubt, rode down this stretch a few days after Drake's failed ambush near Panama; one imagines the Treasurer, feeling relieved, and looking forward to his voyage home to Spain. Baskerville also, still wading, hungry, soaked to the skin without the benefit of horses; would be depressed and worrying about the bad news he would have to relay to Drake at Nombre de Dios.

Overall, progress through the river passage was steady and easy. José and his companions from the other farm, paddling along barefoot more than kept up with the horses. Nearing the end of our ride we left the river before the most southerly of its major 90° bends from west to south (Map E). *Here it is important to note that we had not seen any major tributary flowing into the Nombre de Dios on the east bank all the way from the Pavos junction.*

Having left the river, and crossing some fields we regained our path of the morning walk, then we ascended to the high ground south west of the farm. Was this the route of the Camino I wondered?

Back at the farm, we had taken 1½ hours to return from the Pavos junction. Over refreshing drinks we calculated that the Spaniards would have taken *at least* 5 hours for the journey from the Pavos to Nombre de Dios and back – and effectively ruling out the junction as an ambush site.

After a meal and rest at the farm, we returned to the Juan-Miguel river to complete our task of detecting up to the point where the trail crosses at the ford. José came as well helping with the detection and thoroughly enjoying himself. We found a few more metal objects, but, again, no antiquities. We were naturally disappointed but reason told us that this was hardly justified. This was a meandering tributary of the

*Michael – Juan Miguel River*

*John – Nombre de Dios River*

Nombre de Dios working its way across a flood plain to enter the main river. By erosion and deposition the course must have changed significantly over more than 400 years. We had done our best to examine the shingle banks because we realised that the present river bed would mostly not have been the same in 1573. If there was still a stray silver bar left in the river, after the search by the Spaniards, it would now, no doubt, be buried deep in one of the banks as its heavy weight caused it to sink in the sediment; perhaps out of the range of our present detector, and we had not even been able to examine the banks. We were satisfied that had there been such a heavy metal object, within the range of our detector in the bed of the stretch of the river we had examined, then we would have found it. So in that sense we were content with our effort.

That evening, as on the previous evening, we walked down from the farm to the large bend in the Nombre de Dios river for our wash. A beautiful spot with tall trees and a large flock of egrets chattering in one of the trees where they gathered for the night. This was definitely on the most northerly major bend as the river came from the south and then turned west-north west. We knew, of course, that the Juan-Miguel did not enter the Nombre de Dios on this bend, but it is shown as doing so, on the DMA map we were using.[17] That evening, when chatting to José, we asked him if he knew of an old dam on the River Fato but he had no knowledge of one.

The following morning was our last for ground studies in this area. We would have to leave by mid-day to ensure that we could reach Tocumen Airport, Panama City, in time to meet Sue Jackson due to fly in from Houston in the evening. From the farm we walked across José's fields and all the way up the valley of the Juan-Miguel to the area of Webster's candidate ambush site that we had inspected in 1993. We tried to do some detecting in a section of the river here; this was difficult as it consisted of stagnant pools in this dry season. Nothing was found. As there was a long winding stretch of river to examine, and we had little time available, we gave up. Our memories of 1993 were re-inforced that this area had nothing to commend it as an ambush site.

Returning to the Nombre de Dios river we spent our remaining time examining the area near the northerly major bend. There is a large shingle island in the centre of the river (Map F). Examination of this carefully with the detector showed nothing. On the outside of the bend, under the tree where the egrets nest, is a very deep pool, but we looked at the eastern river bank running south from the bend to see if there were any deep cuts caused by years of mule traffic exiting the river near the bend but before it. Nothing like that is evident near this corner of the river. The Camino must have left the river further upstream.

However, walking across towards the Juan-Miguel along by the fenced trail, which itself is on a raised section of ground, some fairly deep cuts, well grown over, can be observed near where the trail divides at the gate (Map F), just possibly contributing to the idea that the trail had crossed the plain from the south and from the general direction of the farm ridge and had then crossed this slight rise in the ground.

We had done our best to inspect the whole area around the farm feeling very familiar with it. After lunch and taking photographs of José and family to send to them later, we left for Nombre de Dios via the river. Michael rode José's mule together with our rucksacks so giving a good demonstration of its carrying power, while I rode one of José's horses. An easy ride down this now familiar and beautiful stretch of river. This is the lower Nombre de Dios which Webster suggests was probably clogged with debris, fallen trees and sediment in the 16th century making necessary the land crossing for the Camino on the final part of the route.

Thanking José for all his help and hospitality we then hitched a lift in a dusty builder's pickup for the first part of our return journey to Panama City.

# Discussion

Now to draw threads from the records and tie them together with our own observations.

## Distances

Upon return from the 1994 expedition, I studied carefully the aerial photographs on which the DMA map is based and my own photographs of the area around the farm taken from the small plane in 1993. I was very fortunate to have snapped these particularly helpful shots, as at that moment I had never seen the countryside before and did not know what to look for. Together these showed that the farm, on its ridge, is correctly placed on the map in relation to the two major 90° bends in the Nombre de Dios river. Because we had been misled by the position given on the map for its junction with the Juan Miguel, we had originally thought that the farm needed to be marked further south on the map to allow for the space available on the plain which was readily observed by ground studies. Careful study of the aerial photographs confirm the course of the Juan-Miguel as it turns north to the west of relatively higher ground and then westwards, past the ford, to join the Nombre de Dios to the NW of the northerly 90° bend. This area has many trees thus tending to conceal it in aerial photographs. Those drawing the map from the aerial photographs must have been confused by the double fenced trail running across to this same bend, and so took this to be the tributary. Some of the fence posts grow into trees giving very much the look of a river. All of this is readily observed on the ground. A larger scale sketch map of the area has been drawn, Map F.

Being sure of our position as the trail leaves the hill and descends to the plain, allows the complete Camino Real to be sketched from Old Nombre de Dios to the Juan-Miguel river, and so some trail distances to be measured on the map, using a fine cord, so as to follow all the various bends in the trail and give distances "as the foot walks":–

# Table II

| CAMINO REAL | |
|---|---|
| **Approximate walking distances from Nombre de Dios Old City to:** | |
| Juan-Miguel River Ford (Map E) | about 3.5 km or 2.2 miles |
| Southerly major 90° bend in Nombre de Dios River (Map E & G) | about 4.2 km or 2.6 miles |
| "Farm ridge" and then on to Nombre de Dios River (route of our horse-ride) (Map G) | about 4.8 km or 3.0 miles |
| E. Webster's suggestion for entry of Camino into Nombre de Dios River (Map G) | about 6.6 km or 4.1 miles |

**The River Campos**

Is the Juan-Miguel River the River Campos of the Spanish reports, or is there an alternative?

The reports are very clear that the ambush was on land and at the River Campos; this implied a crossing of the Campos by the trail, or in other words they are using the name of the river to denote a point on the trail. Also, quite obviously, the ambush, being on land, occurred before the Camino entered the Nombre de Dios river. Baskerville says that after 1 league on land "you take up the course of ryver for the most part up to the girdell" (see page 12). He inclines to over-estimate distances not surprising over such difficult ground. He did so with later distances; so his first league is unlikely to be more than 3 miles. Baskerville makes clear that the trail was then *in* the river; he fought the Spaniards there, so would hardly forget. The Spaniards would be keen to route the trail into the river as soon as possible as river passage was so much easier. We found this to be so ourselves when riding down the Nombre de Dios on horseback. Interesting light is thrown on this aspect also by the comments of the "Anonymous Jew"; he travelled the Camino in 1620, finally over the section into Porto Belo and of this says:

> "On going in these two rivers you go for more than 7 leagues and it is the best road there is in all the 18 leagues".

The same must have applied to the Pavos and Nombre de Dios river passages.

Hence we have every reason to believe that the Camino entered the Nombre de Dios river within, or no more than, 3 miles along the trail. Accepting this, then there is only one tributary to consider before that point – the Juan-Miguel which therefore is the Campos River.

Webster, in his correspondence with Michael, does state that there is another tributary to the east bank of the Nombre de Dios before its junction with the Pavos, and that this tributary might be the Campos. However, no tributary is marked on the DMA map,[17] and aside from small streams, we did not notice one on our ride down the river (page 42). In any event such a tributary would be higher up the Nombre de Dios from the point of entry of the Camino, thus ruling it out as the ambush would then have been in the river.

Should we take notice of the Spanish accounts which state longer distances of 1½ or 2 leagues? As discussed earlier (see page 22) these longer distances are discredited to some degree; as we see from the above they may now be safely ruled out.

All the above settles the question "which is the Campos River" very satisfactorily.

**Route of the Camino over and beyond the River Campos**

We followed the trail, as I have described, to the River Campos. We were assured that we were following the Camino when we left Nombre de Dios, convinced we were en route, and assured by José at the farm that we had done so. But, is there any alternative? Might not the trail have branched off somewhere, now hidden from view, and crossed the Campos elsewhere?

There is an alternative, by the trail being routed on the higher ground to the east of the plain, which is Webster's suggestion. Then on this eastern side, by way of example, either crossing the Campos near the point marked 9 metres (Map G point X), or much higher up its valley (Map G point Y).

For the first of these possibilities, the trail would need to cross a small section of plain, to the south east of the farm and then cross higher ground south of the farm ridge to enter the Nombre de Dios River at or near the point where we ourselves left in on horseback (Map G point Z). Such a route would provide only a very short section of level plain for the ambush, and of course, we found no sign that the trail had followed the high ground on this east side (see page 34).

The second possibility is that proposed by Webster and was his preferred route. Turning by the Campos as shown (Map G) it then crosses the high ground much further south to enter the Nombre de Dios at 6.6 km (Map G and Table II). Webster's suggestion was based on map study; we took it very seriously before our expeditions. We tried to cover this ground on our first visit and inspected the ambush site involved on both visits. Our ground studies, we feel, counted against this route for several reasons:

Again, there was no sign of any trail on the hills to the east.

An unsatisfactory ambush site – very confined.

Too long a distance for the Spaniards to flee and return in the timescale recorded by Drake.

Too long a distance for Baskerville's first league on land before the trail entered the river.

Therefore, we strongly favour the route whereby the Camino crossed the Campos at the ford, 2.2 miles from old Nombre de Dios. We had taken over an hour on each occasion to walk this distance; perhaps we might have pressed ourselves to travel a little faster, the time would hardly have been less than an hour even so; this is the value of ground studies well demonstrated. Similarly the Spaniards on a familiar trail, one might have thought, could have done it in less. Maybe, but, as we know, they were walking, the trail was difficult and muddy, the time was near mid-day in the greatest heat. We can well understand that the time taken was needed. Once again the longer distances quoted in the Spanish reports are discredited. The distance 2 leagues, led Webster to suggest the Pavos junction as a site. But as we found (pages 41 & 42) it is simply too far away when foot travel is about 2 miles per hour. A 6 mile double journey occupies 5-6 hours, Drake could have buried the silver twice over.

Having crossed at the ford, and run along by the river Campos, which direction does the trail follow across the plain?

This direction is the very line of the ambush. As discussed on page 46 the trail did not seem to turn west, by the present fenced route, so as to enter the Nombre de Dios at the first major bend. Rather, it needed to go on because these major bends, and two more just further upstream were, no doubt, choked with debris in those days as Webster had suggested (see page 46). Across the plain the trail could have followed a south-east direction near the course of the Campos river; south across to the farm ridge, or south-south west angled towards the Nombre de Dios. The first of these can be excluded – why go down the Campos valley when one was aiming to enter the larger river? For the second, the trail would cross the plain reaching the farm ridge and perhaps ascending it by the route of the present path up to the farm – a very well worn old track to the top of the ridge. From the ridge the trail would cross the high ground and then down to enter the river where we had emerged from it on horseback (Map G point Z). Finally, the angle nearer the river, instead of ascending the ridge, would follow through east of the next major bend in the river and then on to enter at the same point. For both of these routes the distance from old Nombre de Dios to the point of river entry is about 3 miles, fitting in very well with Baskerville's "first league".

Revealing light is shed on this question of route by the French account (see page 21) which includes the statement that "silver was interred on a tiny island". There are no islands in the Juan-Miguel river, it is too small, but there are islands in the Nombre de Dios. As heavy silver bars would not be carried very far, this favours the route across the plain nearer the river, and, perhaps more importantly, weighs in heavily against a route for the Camino east of the plain on the higher ground.

**Nature of the terrain at the ambush site**

Would this level ground near the river be too soft for mule traffic?

Webster thought so, which is why he proposed a route for the Camino on higher ground to the east. In contrast we found the plain area to be hard and dry (page 34). Although occupied by numerous cattle, it was well grass-covered and there were no large muddy areas which cattle notoriously create. Sedimentary, and with a gravel content, it seemed to be free-draining. On our first visit, after rain, this was still the situation; whereas the clay path through the hills was slippery. We were there towards the end of the dry season, the same time of year as the ambush.

But was not this plain covered by forest in 1573? In other words it is dry today because the trees have been largely cleared. Here it is interesting to note that the English report tends to suggest a somewhat clearer area along the line of the ambush (p.20). Together with this, the Spanish account described the area as "bush". Another of the observations of our friend the "Anonymous Jew", 1620, now becomes very interesting. On the last stage of his journey before Porto Belo he noted:

"There are in this road many sabanas which are meadows where there are many cows feeding."

So, cattle were being kept, in large numbers, inland from Porto Belo soon after the Camino had changed to the new route. Thus, it would seem reasonable to suppose that cattle were also kept inland from Nombre de Dios in its heyday. However, Antonelli[16] cites as one of the disadvantages of Nombre de Dios that "*of this pasture ground there is great want in Nombre de Dios*". Antonelli was advancing as many reasons as he could to persuade a parsimonious King Phillip II to move the port to Porto Belo. Many cattle were kept inland near the City of Panama in those days, but the Spaniards would hardly have wanted to carry fresh meat on a three-day journey across a hot Camino to supply Nombre de Dios and the large needs of the sailors of the Treasure Fleet who would be avid for fresh food. The present River Fató, the 16th century "Factor's River", runs into Nombre de Dios bay near the former negro town (Map B). The very name of this river, and the fact that a dam was being built on it in 1573, strongly suggests the then use of its valley for agriculture. There is plenty of level ground in this valley, so cattle could have been kept there, not withstanding Antonelli's observation. It is but a short distance from the Fato valley across to the plain of the ambush site. So, perhaps the scene on the plain in 1573 (Map H) could have been similar, if less extensive, to the present scene – the Spaniards keeping cattle on their Campos.

## The Ambush site

Map H shows the area now proposed for the site of the ambush. The two possible routes for the Camino across the plain are shown. Drake and his party would have moved in from the east making their overnight camp on the hill where we found the wild orange trees. Next day, at about 10.30 am, they would move down quietly to about 50 paces from the trail; hiding below the banks of the Campos river or screened by scrub and trees on the fairly open plain. Possibly the English were at the north end near the Campos and the French nearer the south or the Nombre de Dios. Cimmarones would be detailed to halt the mule trains. Silver would have been buried at convenient points in and near both rivers and all across the plain to the east of the trail.

When the Spaniards were approaching, upon return, Drake's party would have reassembled on the hill and then withdrawn across the River Fató in the area where a new dam was being constructed.

## Conclusions

The Camino Real can be traced inland for more than two miles through the hills south of Nombre de Dios to the Juan-Miguel river. Convincing evidence is presented that this is the Campos river of the 16th century. South of the point where the Camino crosses the Juan-Miguel is a plain where we confidently believe the ambush of a 190-mule train by Francis Drake on 29th April 1573 took place. The trail then continues southward to enter the Nombre de Dios river after a total of about three miles.

Our extensive study of the area leaves little doubt that the plain is the ambush site. Could silver still remain buried there, after more than four centuries? This we still do not know. The balance of evidence, discussed in this account, is that some 200 silver bars might have remained, undiscovered, at the time. Of course, over the months following April 1573, muleteers would have been careful to search as they passed the site. There would also be other searches by individuals. But perhaps some bars might have escaped the twin processes of curious probing and exposure by floods. From 1595 onwards the route was abandoned and the Nombre de Dios area returned to the jungle. More than 200 years elapsed before the area was repopulated and local people today have scant knowledge of the 16th century events.

Our limited examination of a stretch of the Juan-Miguel river by metal detector was unproductive but there is still a huge area waiting to be surveyed. A conclusive identification of the site would come from the discovery of any remaining buried silver; this could bear tally-numbers which might be traced back to the episode through the Archives of the Indies in Seville. Such a find would provide a truly remarkable link with a fascinating event in history, the discovery of the lost treasure of Sir Francis Drake!

Further exploration could be directed as follows:

a)    A comprehensive search of the whole area of the ambush site with metal detectors. A team would be required for this extremely worthwhile study. The chance may be lost if treasure hunters were to comb the area. These hunters are already beginning to move in.

b)    Examine the River Fató to see if the site of the 16th century dam can be traced. This would further establish the area of the ambush by indication of the line of approach and return of Drake's party.

c) Look further for the point of entry of the Camino into the Nombre de Dios river. The search under a) could lead to the discovery of 16C artefacts and coins which would establish the route of the trail. A complete map could then be drawn of the first land section of the Camino Real from Nombre de Dios.

# References

1. Sir Francis Drake Revived (London, 1626).
2. Froude, James Anthony, English Seamen in the 16th Century (London, 1895).
3. Corbett, Julian Stafford, Sir Francis Drake (London, 1890).
4. Corbett, Julian Stafford, For God and Gold (based on reference 1).
5. Wright, Irene A., Documents Concerning English Voyages to the Caribbean and the Spanish Main 1569-80 (London, 1932).
6. Mason, A E W, The Life of Sir Francis Drake (London, 1941).
7. Williamson, James A, Sir Francis Drake (London, 1951).
8. Bradford, Ernle, Drake (London, 1965).
9. Thompson, George M, Sir Francis Drake (London, 1972).
10. Sugden, John, Sir Francis Drake (London, 1990).
11. Blashford-Snell, John and Cable, Michael, Operation Drake (London, 1981).
12. Gage, Thomas, The English American (London, 1684).
13. Webster, Edwin C, The Camino Real (1977).
14. Baskerville, Sir Thomas, Discourse (of Sir Francis Drake's Voyage 1595-6) (in Andrews K R (Ed) The Last Voyage of Drake and Hawkins (Cambridge 1972)).
15. Webster, Edwin C, Nombre de Dios, Actas de Simposium Nacional de Antropologia, Arqueologia y Etnohistoria de Panama (1977).
16. Antonelli, Baptista, Nombre de Dios: A relation of the ports, harbours, forts, and cities in the West Indies, 1587 (in Richard Hakluyt, Principal Navigations, London, 1907).
17. Defence Mapping Agency. Nombre de Dios to Palenque 1:12,500 (Washington, 1990).
18. Dampier, William, A New Voyage Around the World (London, 1699).
19. Servicios Geographico E Historico, Carpeta IV Mapa No 66 quoted in Webster, reference 15.
20. Andrews, Kenneth R, Elizabethan Privateering (Cambridge, 1964).
21. Keeler, Mary Freer, Sir Francis Drake's West Indian Voyage 1585-6 (London, 1981).
22. Mathewson, Duncan, Treasure of the Atocha (London, 1986).
23. Maynard, Thomas, His Account (of Sir Francis Drake's Voyage 1595-6) (in Andrews K R (Ed) The Last Voyage of Drake and Hawkins (Cambridge, 1972)).
24. The "Anonymous Jew" Descricion General del Reyno de Pirü (ca 1620) quoted in Webster, reference 13.

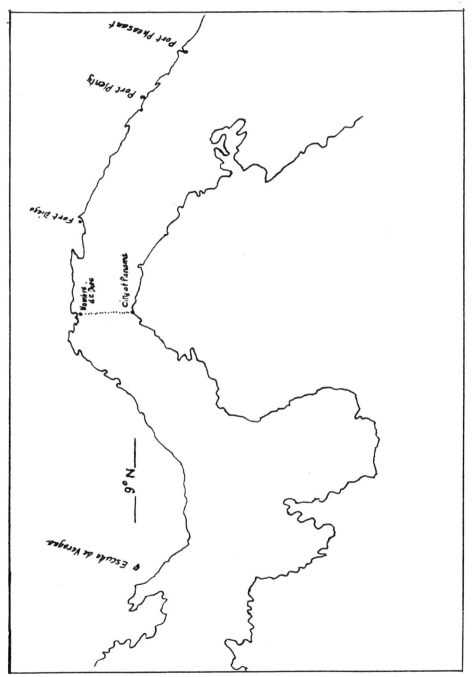

Port Pheasant

Port Plenty

Port Diego

Nombre de Dios

City of Panama

9° N

Escudo de Veragua

*MAP A1 The Isthmus in 1572*

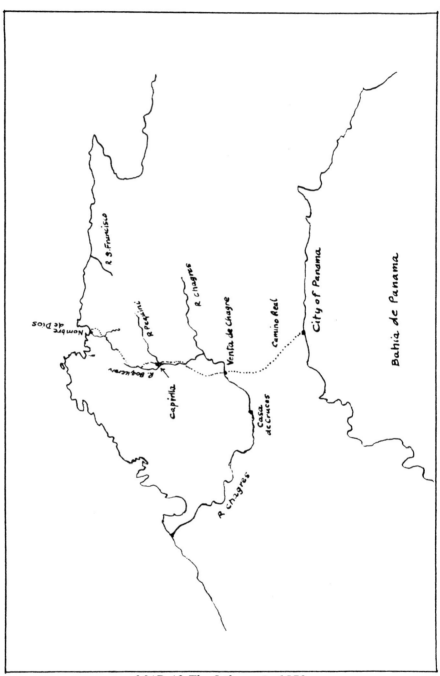

*MAP A2 The Isthmus in 1572*

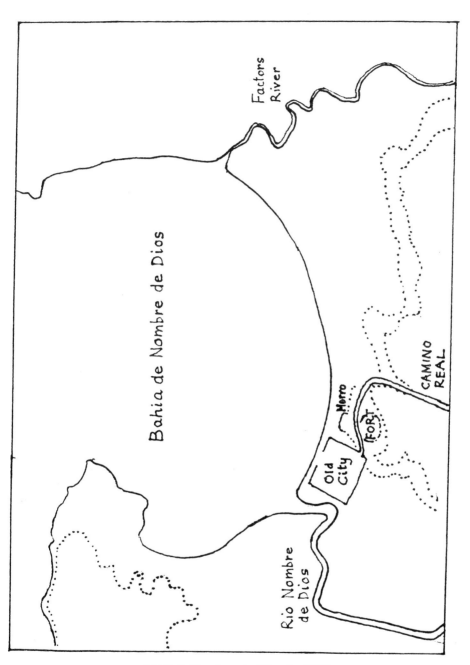

*MAP B Nombre de Dios in 1572*

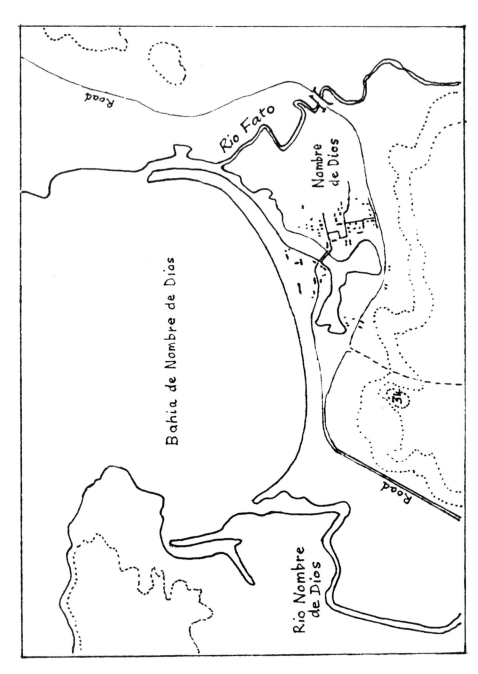

*MAP C Nombre de Dios today*

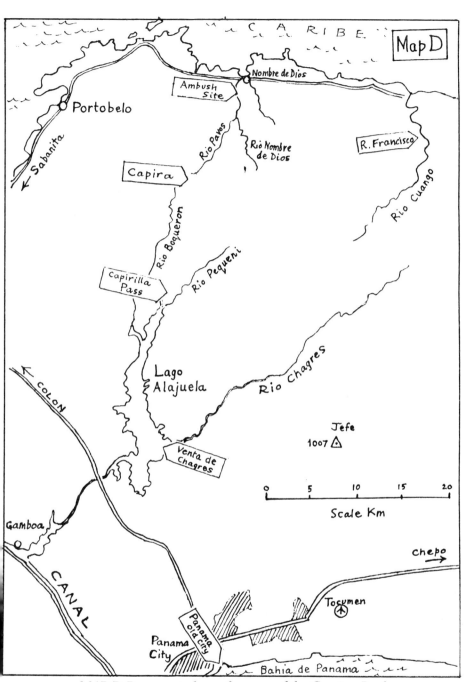

*MAP D Panama today – the area of the Camino Real*

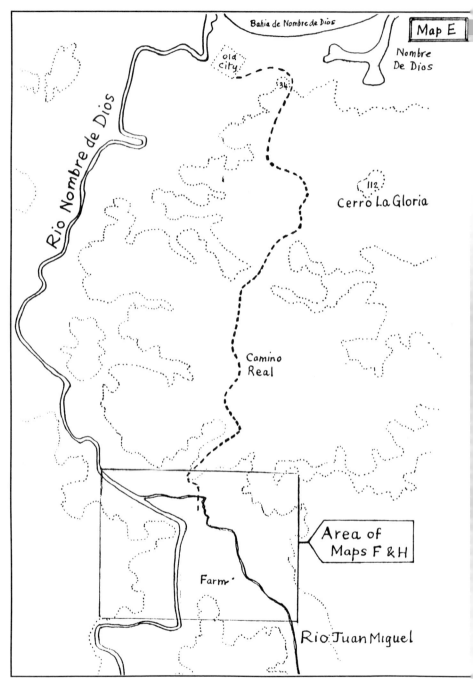

*MAP E Nombre de Dios River – inland*

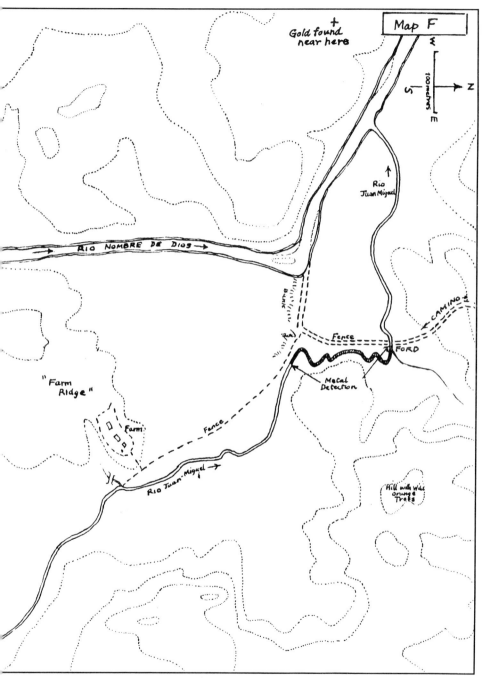

*MAP F Junction of Nombre de Dios and Juan Miguel rivers*

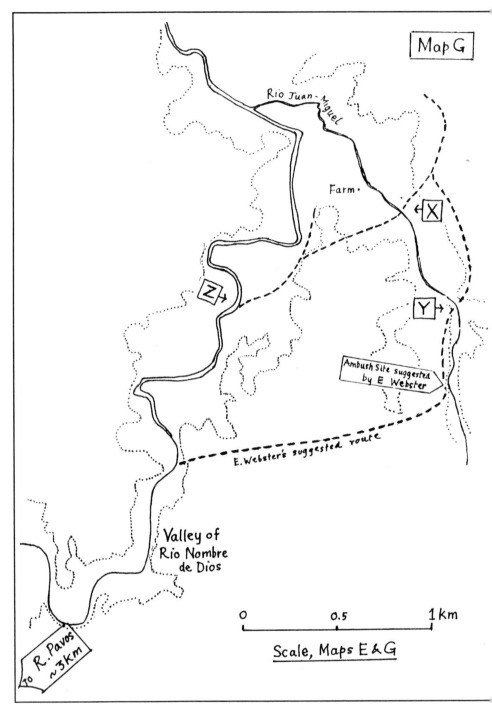

MAP G Nombre de Dios River – further inland

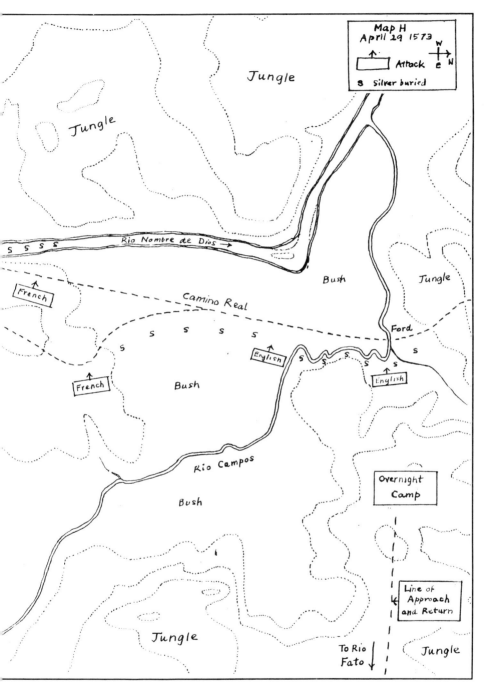

*MAP H The Ambush Site 1573*

# Appendix

Amount and value of Gold and Silver on the Mule Train.

**Gold**  Calculations are based on the amount of gold in the Elizabeth I one pound† coin and on the comparative value of the Elizabeth I pound with the Spanish gold peso*

£1 pound Elizabeth I = 174.5 grains of 22 carat gold

Thus modern value of gold in $\left.\begin{array}{c} \\ \\ \end{array}\right\}$ = $\dfrac{174.5 \times 22 \times 258}{480 \times 24}$ = £86.3
Elizabeth I pound

$\quad\quad\quad$ (NB 1 Troy ounce = 480 grains = £258 in Jan 1994)
$\quad\quad\quad\quad$ 12 Troy ounces = 1lb avoirdupois.)

1 gold peso = 8 shillings Elizabeth I = 8/20 x 174.5 = 70 grains

22 carat gold = £34.5

## Gold on Mule Train

Spaniards recovered 11 gold bars belonging to King valued at 6,300 pesos

1 gold bar value is 573 pesos = $\dfrac{573 \times 70}{480}$ = 83.5 Troy ounces = 7lb

Total gold at 100,000 pesos = $\dfrac{100,000}{573}$ = 174 bars = 1218lb
$\quad\quad\quad\quad\quad\quad\quad$ value (1994) £3,450,000.

1218lb is a full load for 4 mules

## Silver on Mule Train

There were 190 mules. Since 4 were carrying gold, then 186 were carrying silver.

186 carrying 300lb silver bars each = 186 x 300 = 55,800lb or about 25 tons.

Modern value 55,800lb at £42/lb (Jan 1994) = £2,343,600 (Jan 1994).

## Number and Size of Silver Bars

Take 50lb as an example of the weight of 1 bar of silver

Then there were $\dfrac{55,800}{50}$ = 1,116 bars on mule train

Francis Drake buried 15 tons = 33,600lb = $\dfrac{33,600}{50}$ = 672  50lb bars.

Volume of 50lb bar of silver = 2,250 cubic centimetres

So if a bar is 30cm long then width is 7.5cm depth 10cm
$\quad\quad\quad\quad\quad\quad\quad$ or 1 foot x 3" x 4½"

---

\*  Several authors note the gold peso to be about 8 shillings Elizabeth I in the 1570's. John Sugden[10] is one example.

†  Note: the one pound coin *not* the sovereign which was worth 30s in Elizabeth I reign.